Discover the Power of Digital Declutter

Reclaim Your Energy, Focus and Time

DR MEHERNOSH J RANDERIA

Acknowledgement

Writing a book is often seen as a solitary journey, but in truth, it is shaped by the wisdom, encouragement, and unwavering support of many. As I reflect on the journey of bringing *Discover the Power of Digital Declutter* to life, I find myself deeply grateful to those who have been part of this process in ways both seen and unseen.

A special note of heartfelt appreciation to Heena M Shrivastava, my book coach, whose guidance and insights have been invaluable. Your unwavering belief in my work and your ability to refine my ideas have helped shape this book into something meaningful and impactful. Thank you for walking alongside me on this journey and for being a sounding board through every twist and turn.

To my readers – thank you for allowing this book to be a part of your journey. Your reflections, learnings, and takeaways are what truly bring these words to life.

Lastly, my gratitude extends to all those who, in ways big and small, have contributed to my growth as a writer and thinker. Every conversation, every piece of feedback, and every moment of support has added another layer to this work.

Contents

Preface

In a world where digital connections drive both our professional and personal lives, we often find ourselves overwhelmed by **endless notifications, scattered files, overflowing inboxes, and mindless scrolling**. Technology, designed to enhance our lives, has instead become a source of stress, distraction, and mental fatigue. **The problem isn't technology itself—it's how we manage it.**

This book was born out of a simple realization: **digital clutter is just as draining as physical clutter, yet it often goes unnoticed.** We clear our homes and workspaces, but rarely do we pause to organize our digital lives. The hidden cost of digital clutter—lost time, reduced focus, and increased stress—affects us daily, yet few take intentional steps to regain control.

As a Professional Certified Coach (PCC) from the International Coach Federation (ICF), Certified Trainer of Getting Things Done (GTD) and Certified Master Trainer of Neuro-Linguistic Programming (NLP), I have worked with countless individuals and organizations struggling with **information overload and digital burnout**. I've seen firsthand how simple yet structured decluttering techniques can transform not only productivity but also **mental clarity, work-life balance, and overall well-being**.

This book is designed as a **step-by-step guide to digital transformation**—not just by cleaning up your devices but by reshaping the way you interact with technology. Using a combination of **practical strategies, mindful tech habits, and NLP techniques**, you'll learn how to:

- Identify and eliminate digital distractions that waste your time.
- Organize your digital space for better efficiency and mental clarity.
- Use technology **with intention, not out of habit**.
- Reframe your mindset toward digital wellness using **NLP principles**.

Decluttering is **not about restriction; it's about freedom.** It's about regaining control over your technology rather than letting it control you. My hope is that this book will empower you to build a **simpler, clearer, and more focused digital life**, allowing you to dedicate your energy to what truly matters.

Let's begin this journey together—because **when you clean up, you speed up.**

Introduction

Welcome to a New Era of Digital Clarity!

In today's hyper-connected world, our digital lives have become as cluttered as our physical spaces—if not more. Our devices are filled with thousands of unread emails, unused apps, scattered files, and non-stop notifications that demand our attention. This clutter, while seemingly harmless, gradually erodes our productivity, mental clarity, and overall well-being.

You might find yourself constantly distracted, struggling to locate important files, overwhelmed by endless notifications, or drowning in digital noise without even realizing the toll it takes on your focus and efficiency. If this sounds familiar, you're not alone. The digital world was designed for convenience, yet without mindful management, it often becomes a source of stress and inefficiency.

The good news? Just like tidying up a messy room brings relief, organizing your digital space can unlock immense mental clarity, increase your productivity, and allow you to regain control over your time.

Why This Book?

This book, *Discover the Power of Digital Declutter*, is designed to be your *Clutter Cutter Handbook* to enable you to clean up to speed up. It serves as a comprehensive guide to reinforce the practices you've already implemented and help sustain a clutter-free digital life in the long run. Whether you're a professional juggling work-related digital assets, a student managing study materials, or simply someone who wants to use technology more intentionally, this guide will provide actionable steps to:

- Maintain a decluttered digital space.
- Optimize digital workflows for productivity.
- Cultivate mindful digital habits.
- Improve focus, efficiency, and overall digital well-being.

What You'll Learn

In the coming chapters, we'll break down:

- **Why digital decluttering is essential** and the impact clutter has on your cognitive load.
- **The hidden cost of digital clutter**, from wasted time to emotional fatigue.

- **A structured breakdown of key digital decluttering areas** such as apps, notifications, social media, and files.
- **Effective strategies and best practices** for maintaining a clutter-free digital environment.
- **Long-term digital wellness habits** to prevent digital clutter from creeping back.
- **Recommended tools and resources** that simplify digital organization and efficiency.

Who is This For?

This book is for anyone looking to:

- Strengthen habits that reduce digital distractions.
- Increase focus and productivity by keeping their digital space streamlined.
- Develop a minimalist and intentional approach to technology use.

How to Use This Book

Each chapter is structured with insights, actionable steps, and real-world applications. Instead of following a rigid order, you can focus on the areas that resonate most with your needs at any given time. The key is consistency—small, ongoing improvements will lead to long-term success.

Are you ready to reinforce your digital decluttering journey and make it a sustainable habit? Let's dive in!

Why Digital Declutter Matters

Lost in the Noise: A Story We All Know

Imagine this: You just landed your dream project. The excitement is electric, your mind is racing with ideas, and creativity is flowing like never before. You sit down, fingers poised over the keyboard, ready to bring your vision to life.

Then your phone buzzes. A message. You glance at it—just a second, you think.

Ping! Another notification. Just a quick peek.

Ding! An email lands in your inbox—marked 'urgent.' Your brain shifts gears.

Before you know it, **30 minutes are gone**. By the time you refocus, the energy has faded, the inspiration has cooled, and that perfect moment of creative momentum? **Lost.** The deadline inches closer, but your progress is frozen in a web of digital distractions.

Sound familiar?

This is the hidden cost of digital clutter. The overflowing inbox, the endless notifications, and the cluttered desktop – these aren't just minor inconveniences. They are symptoms of a deeper issue, one that slowly erodes your ability to focus, work efficiently, and think clearly. Like an undiagnosed disease, digital overload **steals your productivity, fractures your attention span, and increases stress levels**, making it harder to achieve your goals. It's not just about **too many emails or messy files**—it's about how technology silently drains your focus, steals your time, and leaves you feeling overwhelmed. But here's the good news: **you can take back control.**

Let's explore why digital decluttering isn't just helpful—it's essential for your productivity, creativity, and peace of mind.

How Digital Clutter Affects Your Life

1. **Reduced Productivity:**
    - Searching for misplaced documents or emails wastes valuable time and interrupts workflow.
    - Multitasking between cluttered tabs and apps decreases efficiency.
2. **Increased Stress & Anxiety:**
    - A messy digital environment mirrors a cluttered mind, leading to overwhelm.
    - Unread notifications and overloaded inboxes create a sense of pressure and unfinished tasks.

3. **Decision Fatigue:**
    - Too many digital choices lead to mental exhaustion and slow down decision-making.
    - The constant influx of information makes it harder to focus on what truly matters.
4. **Poor Time Management:**
    - Excessive screen time spent scrolling social media or consuming irrelevant content reduces productivity.
    - Digital distractions prevent deep work and meaningful engagement.
5. **Security Risks:**
    - Outdated files, weak passwords, and unorganized digital spaces increase vulnerability to cyber threats.
    - Sensitive information stored in unsecured locations poses a risk of data breaches.

The Power of Digital Decluttering

A structured approach to digital decluttering not only helps organize files and reduce digital noise but also enhances mental clarity, focus, and overall well-being. Imagine a workspace where:

- Every file is in its proper place and easily accessible.
- Your inbox is streamlined, free from unnecessary emails.
- Notifications are minimized to only what's essential.
- Your social media feeds are intentional, filled with content that truly adds value to your life.

By consciously reducing digital clutter, you create space for efficiency, creativity, and peace of mind. Instead of feeling overwhelmed by a sea of information, you become the master of your digital world.

Why Now?

The longer we ignore digital clutter, the more overwhelming it becomes. With the increasing reliance on technology, developing mindful digital habits is no longer optional—it is essential. Decluttering your digital life today means fewer distractions, enhanced productivity, and improved well-being for the future.

Taking the First Step

Recognizing the impact of digital clutter is the first step toward change. The next chapters will guide you through a structured decluttering process, providing practical steps to help you regain control. Are you ready to clear the digital chaos and reclaim your time? Let's move forward!

THE HIDDEN COST OF DIGITAL CLUTTER

The Silent Drain on Your Time, Energy, and Focus

Digital clutter is more than just a messy inbox or a disorganized desktop—it's a silent drain on your productivity, mental clarity, and overall well-being. Every unnecessary notification, every misplaced file, and every moment spent searching for information adds up to a significant cognitive load. Without realizing it, you may be **losing hours each week**, feeling mentally exhausted, and struggling to stay focused.

Let's explore the **hidden costs of digital clutter**, helping you recognize its impact so you can take control and reclaim your digital space.

1. Mental Overload & Decision Fatigue

- The brain is constantly bombarded with notifications, unread emails, and unnecessary data, leading to exhaustion.
- Too many digital choices deplete mental energy, making it harder to concentrate and make decisions.

2. Productivity Drain & Time Wasted

- Studies show that professionals spend hours each week searching for misplaced files and managing emails.
- A cluttered digital workspace leads to distractions, preventing deep focus and meaningful work.

3. Digital Hoarding & Emotional Weight

- Holding onto thousands of unread emails, unnecessary apps, and outdated documents creates subconscious stress.
- Cluttered digital spaces contribute to feelings of being overwhelmed, anxious, or out of control.

4. Security & Privacy Risks

- Unmanaged files, weak passwords, and unmonitored apps increase the likelihood of security breaches.
- Sensitive information left unsecured or forgotten can lead to identity theft and data leaks.

5. Negative Impact on Well-Being

- Excessive screen time due to unstructured digital habits affects sleep, mental health, and work-life balance.
- The pressure of staying digitally "caught up" leads to unnecessary stress and burnout.

Taking Control of Your Digital Life

- Recognizing these hidden costs is the first step to change.
- The upcoming chapters will guide you through a structured approach to decluttering and creating a balanced digital life.

Let's move forward and take action toward a clutter-free digital world!

Digital Declutter Quotient (DDQ) Assessment

Before you begin decluttering your digital life, it's important to understand how much clutter exists and how it impacts your productivity, focus, and well-being. The **Digital Declutter Quotient (DDQ) Assessment** will help you measure your current state and identify areas that need the most attention.

How to Use This Assessment

This assessment will help you understand your current digital clutter levels and identify areas where you can improve. Rate each statement on a scale of **0 to 5**, where:

0 = Never

1 = Rarely

2 = Occasionally

3 = Sometimes

4 = Often

5 = Always

Be honest with your responses to get an accurate picture.

Section 1: Device Management

1. My phone's home screen is organized, with only essential apps visible.
2. I regularly delete unused apps from my devices.
3. My desktop/laptop has a clean, organized layout without scattered files.
4. I back up important data regularly.
5. I rarely experience storage issues on my devices.

Section 2: Email and Communication Clutter

6. My inbox is organized, and I can quickly find important emails.
7. I unsubscribe from newsletters or updates I no longer read.
8. I have a system to categorize or archive emails effectively.
9. I regularly delete spam or unnecessary emails.
10. I don't feel overwhelmed by the number of unread messages.

Section 3: Social Media & Notifications

11. I have control over my social media usage without mindless scrolling.
12. I have muted or unfollowed accounts that don't add value to my life.
13. I limit notifications to only essential apps.

14. I set boundaries for social media usage, such as time limits.
15. I feel refreshed, not drained, after using social media.

Section 4: Digital Files & Organization

16. My files are neatly organized into folders.
17. I regularly delete duplicate or outdated files.
18. I can easily locate documents without searching for long periods.
19. My photo gallery is organized, and unnecessary images are deleted.
20. I have a cloud storage system or backup to secure my data.

Section 5: Mindful Tech Usage

21. I focus on one task at a time without getting distracted by devices.
22. I schedule specific times to check emails and messages.
23. I can easily unplug from devices without feeling anxious.
24. I have screen-free time daily, especially during meals or before bed.
25. I feel in control of my technology usage rather than controlled by it.

Calculate your Total Score!

Interpretation:

100 – 125: Digital Declutter Pro: You have excellent digital habits, and your tech usage is intentional and organized. Keep up the great work!

75 – 99: ☑ Moderately Clutter-Free: You're doing well, but there's room to improve. Focus on the areas where you scored lower.

50 – 74: ⚠ Clutter Alert: Digital clutter is affecting your focus and productivity. Consider decluttering specific areas like emails or files.

Below 50: Digital Overload Zone: Your digital life might be overwhelming you. Prioritizing a digital decluttering plan will improve your productivity and well-being.

Reflection Questions:

- What patterns did you notice in your responses?
- Which sections had the lowest scores?
- What small changes can you start with today to improve?

Remember: Awareness is the first step to transformation. You are already on the path to a clutter-free digital life!

Next Steps

1. Identify the areas where you scored the highest—these are your biggest problem areas.
2. As you progress through this book, revisit your assessment results and focus on the sections that address your biggest digital clutter challenges.
3. At the end of your decluttering journey, retake the assessment to measure your progress!

Identify Your Digital Clutter Hotspots

Understanding Digital Clutter

Just like a messy physical space can lead to stress and inefficiency, digital clutter creates mental overload and reduces productivity. Digital clutter accumulates over time in various forms—unread emails, unused apps, redundant files, overflowing cloud storage, and an endless stream of notifications. Identifying your digital clutter hotspots is the first step toward reclaiming control over your digital environment.

Common Digital Clutter Hotspots

Digital clutter manifests in different ways. Below are the most common areas where clutter accumulates:

1. **Smartphone Home Screens** – Are your screens cluttered with numerous apps, notifications, and widgets?
2. **Email Inbox** – Do you have thousands of unread emails, unnecessary subscriptions, or spam cluttering your inbox?

3. **Computer Desktop & Files** – Is your desktop filled with unorganized icons, and do you struggle to find files?
4. **Cloud Storage** – Is your Google Drive, Dropbox, or iCloud overloaded with old, redundant files?
5. **Social Media Accounts** – Are your feeds filled with irrelevant content, notifications, and unnecessary followings?
6. **Notifications & Alerts** – Do constant pop-ups and alerts interrupt your focus?
7. **Photo & Video Libraries** – Are you holding onto thousands of duplicate or unnecessary photos and videos?
8. **Apps & Software** – Do you have apps you never use, yet they take up space and slow down your devices?
9. **Bookmarks & Tabs** – Are you guilty of keeping dozens of open tabs and saved bookmarks you never revisit?

How to Identify Your Personal Digital Clutter Hotspots

To effectively declutter, you need to first pinpoint where clutter is accumulating in your digital life. Follow these steps to identify your clutter hotspots:

1. **Perform a Device Scan:** Take a few minutes to open your phone, laptop, and tablet to assess clutter levels.

2. **List Your Top 3 Problem Areas:** Identify the areas that cause you the most frustration or inefficiency.
3. **Check Storage Usage:** Visit your device's storage settings to see which files and apps take up the most space.
4. **Audit Your Email Inbox:** Look at your unread email count and the number of outdated subscriptions.
5. **Review Social Media Habits:** Assess whether your social media usage is intentional or simply a distraction.
6. **Analyze Your Productivity Impact:** Consider which digital distractions waste the most time in your daily routine.

Taking Action: Small Steps Toward Digital Clarity

Once you've identified your clutter hotspots, take small, manageable steps to start decluttering:

- **Prioritize Quick Wins:** Delete unused apps, clear your home screen, and organize your desktop.
- **Unsubscribe & Delete Emails:** Remove yourself from unnecessary email lists and delete outdated messages.
- **Declutter One Folder at a Time:** Start with one category (e.g., documents, downloads, or photos) and gradually organize.

- **Set a Timer:** Dedicate just 10-15 minutes a day to digital decluttering to make it manageable and sustainable.
- **Track Your Progress:** Keep a simple checklist of areas you've decluttered to stay motivated.

Reflection Questions

To reinforce awareness and build better digital habits, take a moment to reflect:

- Which digital clutter hotspot surprised you the most?
- How does digital clutter affect your focus and productivity?
- What is the easiest area for you to declutter, and what feels the hardest?

By identifying and acknowledging your digital clutter hotspots, you set the foundation for a more organized, efficient, and stress-free digital life.

In the next chapter, we'll take a deep dive into clearing one of the most visible clutter areas—your home screen.

Clear Your Home Screen

The Impact of a Cluttered Home Screen

Your smartphone is one of the most frequently used digital devices, and the way you organize it affects your daily efficiency and mental clarity. A cluttered home screen can lead to decision fatigue, distractions, and wasted time as you navigate through unnecessary apps and notifications.

By clearing and organizing your home screen, you create a digital space that is streamlined, efficient, and conducive to productivity.

Why Clearing Your Home Screen Matters

- **Reduces Decision Fatigue:** A clutter-free home screen eliminates the overwhelming choice of multiple apps, allowing you to access essentials with ease.
- **Improves Focus & Efficiency:** A well-organized layout helps you quickly find what you need without distractions.
- **Encourages Intentional Tech Use:** Placing only essential and high-value apps on your home screen minimizes mindless scrolling.

- **Enhances Aesthetics & Mental Clarity:** A visually clean home screen promotes a sense of calm and order.

Steps to Clear and Organize Your Home Screen

Step 1: Assess Your Current Layout

Before making changes, take a moment to analyze your home screen. Ask yourself:

- Do I use all the apps on my home screen regularly?
- Are there redundant or duplicate apps taking up space?
- Are notifications cluttering my screen and causing distractions?

Step 2: Remove Unnecessary Apps & Widgets

- Delete or offload apps that you haven't used in the last month.
- Move non-essential apps to the app drawer or a secondary screen.
- Limit widgets to only those that provide value (e.g., calendar, weather, to-do lists).

Step 3: Organize Apps into Categories

Grouping apps into folders based on purpose makes navigation easier. Suggested categories include:

- **Work & Productivity** (Emails, Notes, Project Management)
- **Finance & Budgeting** (Banking, Investment, Expense Tracking)
- **Health & Wellness** (Fitness, Meditation, Sleep Tracking)
- **Social & Communication** (Messaging, Social Media, Video Calls)
- **Entertainment & Leisure** (Music, Streaming, Podcasts)

Step 4: Keep Essential Apps Accessible

- Place your most-used apps in the **dock** for easy access (e.g., phone, messages, calendar, browser).
- Keep frequently used apps on the first screen, while less-used apps can go in folders or secondary pages.

Step 5: Choose a Calming Wallpaper

- Opt for a minimalist or nature-themed wallpaper to reduce visual clutter.

- Avoid bright, distracting images that can overstimulate the brain.

Step 6: Disable Unnecessary Notifications

- Go to **Settings > Notifications** and turn off alerts for non-essential apps.
- Prioritize notifications for important apps such as messaging, calendar, and reminders.

Sustaining a Clutter-Free Home Screen

- **Review Monthly:** Set a reminder to reassess and clean up your home screen every month.
- **Limit New Apps:** Before downloading a new app, ask yourself if it truly adds value.
- **Use Digital Wellbeing Tools:** Utilize built-in screen time tracking features to monitor app usage and reduce distractions.

Reflection Questions

- How does your new home screen feel compared to before?

- What was the hardest app to remove, and why?
- How do you think a decluttered home screen will impact your daily productivity?

By implementing these steps, you create a home screen that supports intentional tech use, reduces distractions, and enhances your overall digital experience.

Next, we will focus on taming notifications to minimize digital noise and improve focus.

Tame Notifications – Silence the Noise

The Distraction Dilemma

Notifications are designed to capture your attention. While some are useful, many are unnecessary distractions that interrupt focus, increase stress, and reduce productivity. Managing your notifications ensures that your digital environment serves your goals rather than constantly pulling you away from meaningful work.

Why Managing Notifications is Essential

- **Reduces Digital Overwhelm:** Fewer interruptions mean better mental clarity and lower stress levels.
- **Enhances Productivity:** Staying focused on tasks without frequent distractions increases efficiency.
- **Improves Intentionality:** You decide when to check updates instead of being dictated by random alerts.
- **Supports Digital Well-being:** Less screen time and unnecessary engagement lead to a healthier relationship with technology.

Steps to Take Control of Your Notifications

Step 1: Audit Your Current Notifications

- Open your device's **Settings** > **Notifications** and review which apps are sending alerts.
- Identify apps that send frequent, non-essential notifications (e.g., social media, promotions, games).
- Track how often you react to notifications and whether they disrupt your tasks.

Step 2: Disable Non-Essential Notifications

- Turn off notifications for apps that don't require immediate attention.
- Prioritize notifications for essential apps such as **messages, calendar, emails (work-related), and reminders**.
- Disable marketing, shopping, and promotional alerts that serve no real value.

Step 3: Use Do Not Disturb Mode Strategically

- Activate **Do Not Disturb (DND)** during work hours, meetings, or focused deep work sessions.
- Customize DND settings to allow calls from priority contacts or emergency alerts.

- Set up automatic scheduling for DND during bedtime to improve sleep quality.

Step 4: Customize Notification Settings for Key Apps

- **Email:** Use VIP filters to receive alerts only for important contacts.
- **Social Media:** Mute unnecessary group chats and disable push notifications for likes/comments.
- **News Apps:** Set alerts only for breaking news or topics that genuinely interest you.
- **Messaging Apps:** Turn off notifications for non-urgent group conversations.

Step 5: Implement Notification Batching

- Instead of checking notifications continuously, schedule set times to review messages and alerts (e.g., 9 AM, 1 PM, 6 PM).
- Use Focus Modes (on iOS) or Work Profiles (on Android) to separate personal and professional notifications.

Sustaining a Distraction-Free Digital Space

- **Review Monthly:** Regularly assess notification settings to remove new distractions.
- **Be Intentional:** Before enabling a new notification, ask if it genuinely adds value.
- **Use Silence & Vibration Modes:** Keep your phone on silent mode or use vibration sparingly.

Reflection Questions

- How often do notifications pull you away from important tasks?
- Which notifications can you silence today to reclaim focus?
- How does reducing notifications impact your ability to stay present in the moment?

By managing notifications effectively, you create a digital environment that supports focus, well-being, and intentional usage.

Next, we'll dive into how social media clutter affects your mental space and how to declutter your digital social experience.

Detox Social Media & Declutter Accounts

The Social Media Overload

Social media is a powerful tool for communication, learning, and entertainment, but it can also become a source of distraction, comparison, and mental fatigue. Without proper boundaries, social media can take over valuable time and energy, leading to decreased productivity and emotional strain.

Why Decluttering Social Media is Important

- **Reduces Mental Overload:** A curated feed eliminates unnecessary noise and enhances meaningful interactions.
- **Enhances Focus & Productivity:** Less time spent scrolling means more time for priorities and personal growth.
- **Promotes Positive Digital Well-being:** Unfollowing negative or unhelpful accounts improves emotional health.
- **Encourages Intentional Engagement:** Social media should serve your needs, not drain your energy.

Steps to Detox & Declutter Social Media

Step 1: Audit Your Social Media Usage

- Check your screen time report to see how much time you spend on social media daily.
- Reflect on how social media makes you feel—does it inspire or overwhelm you?
- Identify which platforms provide value and which are just distractions.

Step 2: Unfollow & Mute Non-Essential Accounts

- Unfollow accounts that no longer align with your interests or values.
- Mute or hide accounts that clutter your feed with irrelevant content.
- Unsubscribe from unnecessary Facebook groups, LinkedIn pages, or inactive Twitter feeds.

Step 3: Organize Your Social Media Experience

- Use the **favourites or follow priority** feature to highlight meaningful content.

- Create lists or categories for different types of connections (e.g., professional, personal, learning).
- Turn off auto-play for videos to avoid getting sucked into endless scrolling.

Step 4: Set Boundaries for Social Media Consumption

- Schedule specific times to check social media instead of mindlessly opening apps.
- Use app timers to limit daily social media usage (e.g., 30–60 minutes per day).
- Designate screen-free hours, especially before bedtime or during deep work sessions.

Step 5: Clean Up Your Digital Identity

- Review your own social media profiles—delete outdated posts or personal content that no longer represents you.
- Update your bio, profile picture, and professional details to reflect your current self.
- Strengthen privacy settings to protect your information from unwanted exposure.

Sustaining a Healthy Social Media Routine

- **Review Monthly:** Set a monthly reminder to reassess who and what you follow.
- **Be Intentional:** Before following a new account, ask if it genuinely adds value to your life.
- **Engage Meaningfully:** Prioritize real connections and valuable content over passive scrolling.

Reflection Questions

- How do you feel after cleaning up your social media feeds?
- Which platforms add the most value to your life, and which ones drain your energy?
- What new social media habits will you implement moving forward?

By detoxing and decluttering your social media, you regain control over your digital experience, ensuring that your online presence aligns with your values and priorities.

Next, we'll explore how to organize your digital files for a more structured and stress-free digital life.

Organize Your Digital Files

The Challenge of Disorganized Digital Files

Over time, our digital devices become cluttered with random downloads, duplicated documents, unorganized folders, and outdated files. This disorganization leads to wasted time, frustration, and inefficiency when searching for important documents. A well-structured file system saves time, reduces stress, and enhances productivity.

Why Organizing Your Digital Files Matters

- **Improves Efficiency:** Easily locate documents without endless searching.
- **Frees Up Storage Space:** Deleting unnecessary files prevents digital hoarding and optimizes device performance.
- **Enhances Productivity:** A structured filing system simplifies workflow and task management.
- **Boosts Digital Security:** Organized files reduce the risk of losing important data.

Steps to Organize Your Digital Files

Step 1: Assess Your Current Digital Storage

- Identify where your files are stored (laptop, desktop, external drives, cloud storage, etc.).
- Check how much space each storage area is using and which types of files take up the most space.
- List problem areas—messy downloads, duplicate files, cluttered desktop, etc.

Step 2: Declutter & Delete Unnecessary Files

- Start with the **Downloads folder**—delete old and unused files.
- Go through **Desktop files**—remove random documents and shortcuts.
- Identify and delete **duplicate files** using a duplicate finder tool.
- Remove outdated documents, presentations, and media files that are no longer relevant.

Step 3: Establish a Folder Structure

- Create a logical, easy-to-navigate system with broad categories such as:
    - **Work** (Projects, Reports, Presentations)
    - **Personal** (Finance, Health, Travel, Important Documents)
    - **Photos & Media** (Organized by year, event, or subject)
    - **Reference & Learning** (E-books, PDFs, Study Materials)
- Inside each category, use subfolders for better organization (e.g., **Work > Client Projects > Project Name**).

Step 4: Rename Files for Clarity

- Use descriptive, consistent file names that make searching easier (e.g., "2024_Tax_Return.pdf" instead of "Doc123.pdf").
- Adopt a naming convention that works for you, such as YYYY-MM-DD format for chronological sorting.

Step 5: Migrate Important Files to Cloud Storage

- Move essential documents to cloud storage platforms like Google Drive, Dropbox, or OneDrive for easy access and backup.
- Organize cloud storage in the same folder structure as your local files for consistency.

Step 6: Automate Backups & Maintenance

- Set up automatic backups for critical files to avoid data loss.
- Use cloud syncing services to keep documents updated across devices.
- Schedule a monthly file audit to delete and organize new files.

Sustaining a Well-Organized Digital Space

- **Follow the One-Touch Rule:** File documents immediately instead of leaving them in "Downloads" or on the desktop.
- **Review Monthly:** Set a recurring reminder to clean up unnecessary files and reorganize if needed.
- **Keep a Minimalist Approach:** Avoid digital hoarding by regularly assessing file relevance.

Reflection Questions

- How much space did you free up after decluttering your files?
- What challenges did you face while organizing your digital storage?
- How will an organized file system improve your daily workflow?

By implementing these file organization techniques, you'll create a structured and efficient digital workspace that saves time and enhances productivity.

Next, we'll explore how to build mindful tech habits to sustain your digital decluttering journey.

Build Mindful Tech Habits

The Need for Mindful Technology Use

Technology is an integral part of modern life, but without intentional habits, it can become a source of distraction, stress, and inefficiency. Developing mindful tech habits helps you create a balanced relationship with your digital devices, ensuring that they serve your needs rather than control your time.

Why Mindful Tech Habits Matter

- **Enhances Focus & Productivity:** Reduces distractions and helps you stay engaged in meaningful tasks.
- **Promotes Digital Well-being:** Reduces screen fatigue and fosters healthier technology use.
- **Encourages Intentionality:** Ensures technology is used as a tool for growth rather than mindless consumption.
- **Supports Work-Life Balance:** Helps create boundaries between digital and offline time.

Steps to Build Mindful Tech Habits

Step 1: Implement the One-Task Rule

- Focus on **one task at a time** instead of juggling multiple apps or browser tabs.
- Close unnecessary tabs and apps before starting a task.
- Use **focus timers** like the Pomodoro Technique to maintain deep work sessions.

Step 2: Set Scheduled Check-ins for Emails & Messages

- Avoid checking emails or messages continuously throughout the day.
- Designate **specific times** (e.g., morning, midday, and evening) to process messages.
- Turn off email push notifications to prevent unnecessary distractions.

Step 3: Track & Reduce Screen Time

- Use built-in tools like **Digital Wellbeing (Android)** or **Screen Time (iOS)** to monitor usage.
- Identify the apps consuming most of your time and set **daily usage limits**.

- Aim to reduce screen time by at least **20% per week** by replacing unnecessary digital activities with real-world engagement.

Step 4: Establish No-Screen Zones & Times

- Set **device-free hours** before bedtime to improve sleep quality.
- Avoid screens during **meals, social interactions, and morning routines** to stay present.
- Consider a **weekly digital detox day** where you minimize unnecessary screen usage.

Step 5: Curate Your Digital Consumption

- Be intentional about the content you consume—**unfollow accounts that don't add value**.
- Replace mindless scrolling with purposeful reading, learning, or creative activities.
- Use browser extensions to **block distracting websites** during work hours.

Step 6: Utilize Focus & Productivity Tools

- Use apps like **Forest, Freedom, or RescueTime** to help limit distractions.
- Activate **Do Not Disturb or Focus Mode** on your phone to silence non-essential alerts.
- Use task management tools like **Notion, Trello, or Todoist** to structure your digital workflow efficiently.

Use NLP Anchoring to Reinforce Positive Digital Habits

Anchoring is an NLP technique that links a specific emotional state to an external trigger. You can use this method to associate digital decluttering with a sense of clarity and control.

- Example: Each time you **clear unnecessary tabs or close distracting apps**, take a **deep breath and smile**. This creates a positive reinforcement loop, making decluttering an automatic, satisfying action.
- Over time, your mind will link the action of decluttering with a sense of relief, making it easier to maintain the habit.

Sustaining Mindful Tech Habits

- **Review Weekly:** Reflect on your digital habits and adjust them for improvement.
- **Be Intentional:** Before using a device, ask yourself, *"Is this necessary right now?"*
- **Celebrate Progress:** Small changes add up—acknowledge your wins in reducing digital distractions.

Reflection Questions

- Which tech habits are currently helping or hurting your focus?
- What is one habit you can implement today to reduce digital distractions?
- How will a mindful approach to technology improve your overall well-being?

By developing mindful tech habits, you gain control over your digital life, ensuring that technology enhances your productivity and well-being rather than consuming your time.

Next, we'll explore how to craft a long-term digital wellness plan to maintain balance.

Craft Your Digital Wellness Plan

Why You Need a Digital Wellness Plan

A clutter-free digital life isn't just about a one-time cleanup—it's about **creating a sustainable system** that ensures ongoing digital well-being. Just like maintaining a healthy diet or exercise routine, your relationship with technology requires regular attention and intentional habits.

The Benefits of a Digital Wellness Plan

- **Prevents Digital Clutter from Creeping Back:** Establishes a structured approach to maintaining order.
- **Supports Productivity & Mental Clarity:** Reduces distractions and helps you stay focused on what matters.
- **Encourages Work-Life Balance:** Sets clear boundaries between digital use and personal time.
- **Promotes Healthy Technology Habits:** Ensures that digital tools serve your goals rather than consuming your time.

Steps to Create Your Digital Wellness Plan

Step 1: Define Your Digital Priorities

- Identify how you want technology to serve you—**productivity, creativity, learning, or relaxation**.
- List the most important digital habits you want to maintain (e.g., **organized files, minimal notifications, mindful social media use**).
- Clarify what digital distractions you need to minimize (e.g., **excessive scrolling, unnecessary emails, redundant apps**).

Step 2: Set Digital Boundaries

- **Establish No-Tech Zones:** Keep devices out of the bedroom, dining area, or other personal spaces.
- **Schedule Screen-Free Time:** Designate periods where you unplug from devices, such as **before bedtime or during social interactions**.
- **Define Work vs. Personal Device Use:** If possible, use separate devices for work and personal life to maintain boundaries.

Step 3: Implement a Routine for Digital Maintenance

- **Weekly Check-Ins:** Spend **15-30 minutes every week** decluttering emails, files, and apps.
- **Monthly Deep Clean:** Dedicate time once a month to review storage, organize photos, and update security settings.
- **Quarterly Digital Detox:** Take a step back every few months to assess your overall digital habits and adjust where needed.

Step 4: Optimize Your Digital Environment

- Use **productivity tools** like task managers (Notion, Trello) and focus apps (Forest, Freedom) to streamline digital use.
- Organize your **desktop and folders** with a clear system to avoid future clutter.
- Utilize **cloud storage and backups** to ensure essential data is always accessible and protected.

Step 5: Monitor & Adjust for Continuous Improvement

- Set **reminders** to evaluate your digital wellness every few weeks.
- Reflect on what's working and where you need to improve—are distractions still creeping in?
- Adjust strategies as needed to align with changing priorities and new challenges.

Reframe Digital Decluttering as a Growth Opportunity

Reframing is an NLP technique that shifts the way you perceive an event or habit. Instead of viewing digital decluttering as a **boring task**, reframe it as a **powerful opportunity to reclaim time and mental energy**.

- Instead of saying: *"I have to clean my inbox,"* explore saying: *"I am organizing my digital space to make my work easier and stress-free."*
- This simple language shift transforms decluttering from a chore into a rewarding and empowering habit.

Sustaining a Balanced Digital Life

- **Stay Intentional:** Regularly assess if your digital habits align with your goals.
- **Adapt & Evolve:** Technology changes, and so should your digital wellness plan.
- **Celebrate Progress:** Acknowledge small wins in maintaining a clutter-free and balanced digital lifestyle.

Reflection Questions

- What digital habits do you need to reinforce to maintain digital clarity?
- How can you make your digital wellness plan more sustainable?
- What immediate steps can you take today to start integrating this plan into your life?

By crafting a personalized digital wellness plan, you ensure that your decluttering efforts remain effective long-term.

Next, we'll explore practical decluttering strategies that can be applied in daily life to maintain a streamlined digital environment.

Practical Decluttering Strategies

Clean Up to Speed Up

Decluttering your digital space isn't just about aesthetics—it's about **boosting efficiency, productivity, and mental clarity**. A well-organized digital environment allows you to work faster, reduce distractions, and make better use of your time. By applying practical decluttering strategies, you create a digital system that supports, rather than hinders, your daily activities.

Why Practical Decluttering Strategies Matter

- **Saves Time & Effort:** A streamlined system means no more digging through files or searching for apps.
- **Reduces Decision Fatigue:** Fewer digital distractions lead to better focus and improved decision-making.
- **Enhances Device Performance:** Less clutter means faster load times and smoother device operation.
- **Supports Mental Clarity:** A clean and organized digital space promotes peace of mind.

Actionable Decluttering Strategies

1. The 3-Click Rule for File Organization

- If it takes more than **three clicks** to find a file, it needs better organization.
- Use a clear folder structure such as **Work, Personal, Finances, Learning, and Media**.
- Create subfolders as needed, but keep the hierarchy simple.

2. The 30-Day App Rule

- Delete apps you **haven't used in the last 30 days**—they are likely unnecessary.
- Organize frequently used apps on the home screen and move others into categorized folders.
- Use web-based tools instead of apps when possible to reduce clutter.

3. Inbox Zero Approach

- Unsubscribe from newsletters and spam emails that no longer serve you.
- Set up **email filters and labels** to automatically sort incoming messages.
- Schedule **two dedicated times per day** to check emails instead of constant monitoring.

4. Declutter Your Browser for Better Focus

- Limit open tabs to a maximum of **5-7 at a time**.
- Use **bookmark folders** to save articles instead of leaving tabs open.
- Install productivity extensions like **OneTab** to consolidate and save tabs for later.

5. Weekly Downloads Folder Cleanup

- Schedule a **weekly cleanup** of your downloads folder to avoid unnecessary file buildup.
- Move important files to their designated folders and delete the rest.
- Empty the **recycle bin/trash** regularly to free up space.

6. Optimize Cloud Storage Usage

- Store essential documents in the cloud (Google Drive, Dropbox, OneDrive) for easy access.
- Set up **automatic backups** to prevent data loss.
- Regularly **audit and delete** outdated cloud files to keep storage optimized.

7. Implement Digital Detox Days

- Designate a **screen-free day** or **no-social-media hours** every week.
- Use this time for activities like reading, journaling, or spending time outdoors.
- Track how you feel after reducing digital consumption—it often leads to increased mindfulness.

Sustaining Practical Decluttering Habits

- **Set Monthly Maintenance Reminders:** A small effort each month prevents digital clutter from accumulating.
- **Use Decluttering Tools:** Apps like **CCleaner, Unroll.me, and Clean Email** help automate digital cleanup.

- **Create an Accountability System:** Pair up with a friend or colleague to keep each other on track.

Reflection Questions

- Which decluttering strategy resonated with you the most?
- What is one quick decluttering action you can take right now?
- How will a clean digital environment enhance your productivity and well-being?

By applying these practical decluttering strategies, you can maintain a clutter-free digital life that enhances productivity and peace of mind.

Next, we'll explore how to establish long-term digital wellness habits to ensure sustainable success.

Creating Long-Term Digital Wellness

Why Long-Term Digital Wellness Matters

A one-time decluttering session can create temporary relief, but true **digital wellness** comes from sustainable habits. The key is **consistency, awareness, and routine maintenance** to prevent digital clutter from creeping back into your life.

The Benefits of Long-Term Digital Wellness

- **Reduces Digital Overload:** Keeps devices organized and easy to navigate.
- **Enhances Mental Clarity:** Fewer distractions allow for better focus and productivity.
- **Encourages a Healthy Relationship with Technology:** Helps maintain a balance between online and offline activities.
- **Improves Digital Security:** Regular maintenance ensures your data remains protected and up to date.

Steps to Maintain Long-Term Digital Wellness

1. Conduct Regular Digital Check-Ins

- Set a **weekly reminder** to clear unnecessary files, emails, and apps.
- Monthly, review cloud storage and delete outdated files.
- Every **six months**, do a deep clean of all digital spaces—emails, social media, and local storage.

2. Set Digital Boundaries

- Define **"No-Screen" Zones** in your home, such as the bedroom or dining table.
- Establish **work-life balance** by setting clear times for checking emails and messages.
- Use **focus modes or app blockers** to prevent excessive digital consumption.

3. Automate Maintenance Where Possible

- Use **auto-delete features** for old emails and junk files.
- Enable **cloud backups** for essential files and data security.

- Schedule **automated updates** for apps and operating systems to keep devices optimized.

4. Adopt a Minimalist Approach to Digital Consumption

- Before downloading a new app, ask: *Do I truly need this?*
- Limit the number of social media platforms and focus only on those that provide value.
- Regularly **unfollow or mute accounts** that no longer align with your interests.

5. Prioritize Digital Well-Being

- Use screen time tracking tools to monitor daily and weekly usage.
- Set **intentional goals** for device usage, such as limiting social media to 30 minutes per day.
- Schedule **tech-free time** to reset and recharge, such as a weekend unplugging challenge.

Use Visualization to Maintain a Clutter-Free Digital Space

Visualization is a powerful NLP tool that helps reinforce habits by mentally experiencing success before it happens.

- Close your eyes and **visualize your ideal digital workspace**—a clean desktop, an organized email inbox, and notifications under control. Imagine how that feels.
- Future pace yourself: Picture yourself **six months from now**, maintaining these habits effortlessly. How much easier is your daily workflow? How much calmer do you feel?
- By mentally experiencing the benefits beforehand, you train your subconscious mind to sustain long-term digital clarity.

Sustaining a Healthy Digital Lifestyle

- **Review & Adjust Regularly:** Digital wellness is an evolving process—adapt your strategies as needed.
- **Stay Conscious of Digital Overload:** When you feel overwhelmed, pause and reassess your digital habits.
- **Celebrate Your Progress:** Acknowledge small wins in maintaining a clutter-free and mindful digital space.

Reflection Questions

- What areas of your digital life still need improvement?
- How can you integrate digital wellness practices into your daily routine?
- What long-term digital habits will help you stay in control of your online world?

By committing to long-term digital wellness, you create a sustainable and balanced approach to technology, ensuring a clutter-free and productive digital experience.

Next, we'll explore essential tools and resources to support your journey.

Tools & Resources

Essential Tools for Digital Decluttering

Managing digital clutter can be overwhelming, but the right tools can simplify the process. Below are some of the best apps and platforms to help you organize, automate, and maintain a clutter-free digital life.

1. Email Management

- **Unroll.Me** – Easily unsubscribe from unwanted emails and organize subscriptions.
- **Clean Email** – Bulk delete old emails and automate inbox cleaning.
- **SaneBox** – AI-powered filtering to prioritize important emails.

2. File & Cloud Organization

- **Google Drive / Dropbox / OneDrive** – Cloud storage solutions for file accessibility and backup.

- **Evernote / Notion** – Note-taking and organization tools to keep important information structured.
- **CCleaner** – Removes junk files, duplicates, and unnecessary system clutter.

3. Social Media Management

- **JOMO (Joy of Missing Out)** – Helps reduce social media usage and build healthier screen habits.
- **Hootsuite / Buffer** – Schedule posts and manage multiple accounts efficiently.
- **Feedly** – Organizes news and content into a streamlined reading list.

4. Screen Time & Focus Tools

- **Freedom** – Blocks distracting websites and apps to improve productivity.
- **Forest** – Encourages focus by rewarding screen-free time.
- **RescueTime** – Tracks and analyzes your digital habits to optimize productivity.

5. Security & Privacy

- **1Password / LastPass** – Secure password managers for organizing login credentials.
- **Bitwarden** – Open-source password management tool for digital security.
- **NordVPN / ExpressVPN** – Encrypts internet traffic and enhances online privacy.

6. Task & Time Management

- **Todoist / Trello** – Organizes tasks, projects, and deadlines effectively.
- **Google Calendar / Microsoft Outlook** – Helps schedule and prioritize tasks efficiently.
- **Pomodone / Focus Booster** – Implements the Pomodoro technique to maintain concentration.

How to Choose the Right Tools for You

- **Assess Your Needs:** Identify which areas of digital clutter cause the most stress.
- **Start Small:** Introduce one tool at a time and gradually integrate them into your routine.

- **Automate Where Possible:** Leverage AI and automation to reduce manual decluttering efforts.

Reflection Questions

- Which tool can help you declutter most effectively?
- How can automation improve your digital organization?
- What additional tools do you already use that contribute to digital wellness?

By integrating these tools into your digital decluttering routine, you can simplify organization, boost productivity, and maintain long-term digital wellness.

Next, we'll conclude with key takeaways and actionable next steps.

Final Thoughts & Next Steps

The Journey to Digital Clarity

You've now taken significant steps toward achieving a clutter-free digital life. By identifying digital clutter hotspots, organizing your files, managing notifications, and cultivating mindful tech habits, you've set the foundation for lasting digital wellness.

However, decluttering is not a one-time event—it's an ongoing process. Just as physical spaces require regular cleaning and maintenance, so does your digital environment. The key is to remain intentional and committed to sustaining these habits over time.

Key Takeaways

- **Awareness is the First Step:** Identifying digital clutter allows you to take proactive steps toward reducing it.
- **Small Changes Create Big Impact:** Even minor adjustments, like organizing your home screen or limiting notifications, can greatly improve focus and efficiency.

- **Consistency is Essential:** Regular maintenance prevents digital clutter from creeping back.
- **Technology Should Work for You, Not Against You:** Your digital space should support your goals and well-being, not distract or overwhelm you.

Next Steps: Keeping Up the Momentum

1. Set a Digital Declutter Routine

- Schedule a **weekly check-in** to remove unnecessary files, apps, and emails.
- Plan a **monthly deep clean** to organize folders, manage cloud storage, and streamline digital tools.
- Establish a **quarterly review** to reassess and refine your digital habits.

2. Apply the "One In, One Out" Rule

- Before downloading a new app or subscribing to a new service, ask yourself if it truly adds value.
- When adding a new digital tool, remove an outdated or redundant one to prevent unnecessary accumulation.

3. Share Your Learnings

- Encourage family, friends, or colleagues to join you in creating a clutter-free digital space.
- Discuss the benefits of digital decluttering and share useful tools or strategies.
- Consider hosting a **decluttering challenge** in your workplace or community to inspire collective action.

4. Stay Curious and Keep Learning

- Explore books, podcasts, or articles on digital minimalism and productivity.
- Stay updated on the latest tools and best practices for maintaining a streamlined digital life.
- Reflect on how digital decluttering has improved your efficiency, well-being, and focus.

Aligning Your Digital Space with Your Mindset

Your external digital space reflects your internal state. Through **NLP techniques like anchoring, reframing, and visualization**, you've not only decluttered your devices but also reprogrammed your mindset to sustain long-term clarity.

- Take a moment to reflect: *How does your digital space feel now compared to when you started?*
- What **one NLP technique** will you continue using to maintain digital wellness?

By integrating these NLP strategies into your digital decluttering journey, you ensure that your technology serves you—rather than the other way around.

Your Digital Wellness Commitment

Take a moment to reflect on how far you've come. Now that you've learned strategies to declutter and maintain digital wellness, it's time to **revisit your DDQ Assessment.**

- How has your score improved?
- Which areas have seen the most transformation?
- What habits will you continue to reinforce?

Your digital wellness is a journey, not a destination. By staying intentional and consistent, you can ensure that technology enhances your life rather than overwhelming it. **Now, take a deep breath, embrace your digital clarity, and move forward with purpose!**

Also, take a moment to write down a **personal commitment statement** for your digital wellness. Example:

"I commit to maintaining a clutter-free digital space by regularly organizing my files, limiting distractions, and using technology with intention. My digital environment will support my goals, enhance my focus, and contribute to my well-being."

Final Words

Decluttering your digital life is about more than just deleting files or organizing folders—it's about **taking control of your digital experience** and using technology in a way that aligns with your values and goals. By staying intentional and consistent, you'll enjoy a more focused, productive, and stress-free digital world.

Thank you for embarking on this journey. Now, take a deep breath, enjoy your newfound digital clarity, and move forward with purpose!

About The Author

Dr Mehernosh J Randeria is a distinguished **NLP Master Trainer** and an **ICF-accredited Coach**, widely recognised for his groundbreaking contributions in the field of **Neuro-Linguistic Programming (NLP)** and personal transformation. As the **Founder of W3 Success Academy**, Dr Mehernosh is **India's only Wealth Wisdom Wellness Coach**, advocating a **holistic approach to success** - one that extends beyond financial prosperity to encompass mental, emotional, physical, and spiritual well-being.

Driven by an unwavering mission to unlock human potential, he empowers individuals to **bridge the gap between knowledge and action** through robust NLP methodologies. His unique **Learn-Do-Teach** approach reflects his deep-rooted passion for **lifelong learning, practical application, and sharing wisdom**.

As a **Chartered Accountant** with **almost 2 decades of rich corporate experience** in senior leadership roles, and **another decade plus of intense coaching and training experience** thereafter, he kept his never-ending learning curve always high and the implementation curve even higher, and has made his mark as **one of the finest coaches in the country**.

More Books By The Author

https://thoughtfullyyours.in/

Inspiration is just the beginning—transformation happens when you take action. What if a single quote could challenge your thinking, shift your perspective, or open the door to new possibilities?

In Thoughtfully Yours, India's only W3 Coach and NLP Master Trainer Dr Mehernosh J Randeria presents 99 original thought-provoking quotes along with powerful questions — designed to inspire deep reflection and meaningful action,

Whether you use it for daily reflection, coaching conversations, or as a thoughtful gift, Thoughtfully Yours serves as your personal guide to turning insights into action.

A must-have for personal growth seekers, coaches, leaders, and lifelong learners.
Start your journey today—because the right question can change everything.

https://amzn.to/3QQ9EFb

What is that one thing that stops you from creating the life that you want to live? Do you need more self-compassion? Do you need to feel the need to have more self-worth? How can you increase positivity in all areas of your life?

Imagine how it might feel to dive into life and pursue your true potential. You have the opportunity at any moment to take hold of your life in order to create the structure that works for you. This book gives you the tools that can help you begin to make changes in your life. By integrating six simple yet powerful practices in your life, you will find yourself coming out of your shell in new ways. You will love yourself in ways that make you feel confident, worthy and grateful.

Learning about and applying self-compassion can revolutionize your lifestyle and help you live your very best life. When you truly embrace yourself, you embrace life with excitement and gratitude.

Unlock Lifelong Learning & Growth in Wealth, Wisdom & Wellness with Online Courses from W3 Success Academy

https://www.W3SuccessAcademy.com/Courses

Transform your financial, mental, emotional, physical, and spiritual well-being with expert-led courses. Step into a world of continuous education and personal mastery today!

Some of the most popular courses:

→ NLP Practitioner

→ NLP Master Practitioner

→ High Impact Performer

→ W3 Champion Series

→ Self-ISHQ Challenge

→ Design Your Year Challenge

→ Momentum Mastery Bundle

Follow / Subscribe for regular updates

Weekly Newsletter:
NLP Around You
www.W3Coach.com/nlparoundyou/

W3 Coach Blog
www.W3Coach.com/blog

Facebook
@MehernoshW3

Instagram
@MehernoshW3

LinkedIn
@MehernoshW3

YouTube
@MehernoshW3

X
@mehernoshw3

www.ingramcontent.com/pod-product-compliance
Lightning Source LLC
LaVergne TN
LVHW021144160826
845679LV00023B/2035

* 9 7 9 8 8 9 7 4 4 5 1 5 8 *